The Game of Boxes

Winner of the 2012 James Laughlin Award
of the Academy of American Poets

The James Laughlin Award is given to commend and support
a poet's second book. It is the only second-book award for
poetry in the United States. Offered since 1954, the award
was endowed in 1995 by a gift to the Academy from the Drue
Heinz Trust. It is named for the poet and publisher James
Laughlin, who founded New Directions Publishing Corp.

Judges for 2012
April Bernard
Cyrus Cassells
Dana Levin

The Game of Boxes

[Poems]

Catherine Barnett

Graywolf Press

This publication is made possible in part by a grant provided by the Minnesota State Arts Board, through an appropriation by the Minnesota State Legislature from the Minnesota general fund and its arts and cultural heritage fund with money from the vote of the people of Minnesota on November 4, 2008, and a grant from the Wells Fargo Foundation Minnesota. Significant support has also been provided by the National Endowment for the Arts; Target; the McKnight Foundation; and other generous contributions from foundations, corporations, and individuals. To these organizations and individuals we offer our heartfelt thanks.

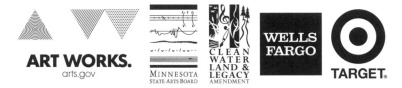

Special funding for this title has been provided by the Jerome Foundation.

Published by Graywolf Press
250 Third Avenue North, Suite 600
Minneapolis, Minnesota 55401

www.graywolfpress.org

Published in the United States of America

ISBN 978-1-55597-620-0

2 4 6 8 9 7 5 3

Library of Congress Control Number: 2012936220

Cover design: David Wells Design

Cover art: Dr. Ida Mann, a pioneer of British ophthalmology, studied the irises of 139 species from the London Zoo. Her drawings, and an essay on "Iris Pattern in the Vertebrates," were published in 1931 by the Zoological Society of London. The cover image is from Plate XX and includes: 1. Typical mammalian iris-circulation. 2. Mohol bushbaby iris. 3. Human iris. 5. Phalanger iris. 6. Rabbit iris. 7. Albino guinea-pig iris. 8. Typical avian iris-circulation. 9. Albino jackdaw iris. 10. Scops owl iris. 11. Bateleur eagle iris. 12. Rockhopper penguin iris. Photograph by Bill Stanton.

Contents

Endless Forms Most Beautiful

Of All Faces

The Modern Period

The Game of Boxes

Endless Forms Most Beautiful

Scavenger Hunt

Can we make a game of it,
race across the yard
and collect the trash?

Shake flowers from bushes,
scare birds from the grass—

Can I write a play of it,
starring Father of Styrofoam!
Mother of Glass!

Chorus

We want to know the reasons for everything
but the mothers tell us *be patient.*
Hey there sweetheart, they say.
A little fortitude, a little patience.

The mothers have beautiful old lady legs.
The silence in them spills into us,
we are as shhhh as we can be.

Chorus

Should we take notes,
before it's over?

We sit beside them,
waiting.

They tell us what's to come that never does come
and we mark it down.

Or they don't tell us but we try to remember it.
Even when the radiator clangs

and the wind blows and the hours
disappear,

they swear we're fine,
we're resilient,

they march us up the stairs
and say we have to laugh about it,

ha ha. We like to laugh,
we're still trying to understand

the story, the one we're in right now.
We thought it would end a little sooner

so we only packed our mouths,
the ones with the mouths singing from them.

Chorus

Every night cars drive by with windows,
buses filled with windows fly right by,
windows filled with windows head home and away from home,
windows opening,
windows closing,
windows in suits and ties
wearing the eyes of strangers or stars.

Chorus

What's wrong? we ask.
To keep from answering, they keep reading.

The Book of Illusions,
The End of Illusion,

and *On Not Being Able to Sleep.*
But we know more than they think.

It's true they love us,
more than anything,

and their hands in the Easter air look loving
moving the eggs to their places.

They hide them over and over again—
under the lion mask,

in the brim of the policeman's hat—
so we'll think there's plenty.

Often the dye seeps into the cracks
and stains the white of the egg,

but so what.
A little salt and it's sweet again.

Old Story

The clock doesn't have an amygdala
so it doesn't worry, it tells
its own quick trickle-down story
of now and now and now until
neither yesterday nor tomorrow
is where it should be.
Welcome, traveler!
You might as well stay a while
and kneel to Happiness
and its hymns and its cross.

To Speak of Other Things

Only the garden tells the truth
though it was left a little flayed,
cut down,

left a little shut down and fenced in and stunned,
in its place he left dirt,
dog fence, sumac, holes,

in his place he left gardens
wanting what a garden always wants,
everything back in order and in bloom.

Night Hour

All night the unlocked door
remains unlocked,
all night it rocks in its frame
and speaks to the child who waits
in his bed with only a pillow
and a phone under it—

and no light in the house,
no other sound in a house
left open to mothers, thieves, wind—

Categories of Understanding

I'm studying the unspoken.
"What?" my son asks.
"What are you looking at?"
But there is no explaining,
I can only speak the way light
falls, the way the cotton sheet
lays itself over his sleeping or resting
or dissolving body, touching him with
its ephemera, its oblivion.

Underground Sublime

I heard myself calling into
the crowded subway,
hold the doors!
Everything I cared about
was already inside
and the voice I discovered then
is like the siren now outside
my window, the manhole cover
knocking again and again
as cars drive across it,
voice of the nights'
adrenaline crow
calling from the rooftops
into avenues of air.

Textbook & Absence (Anatomy)

At school he studies the human body:
aorta, valve, muscle, vein.
At home he redesigns it
out of cardboard and twine
until it looks like a coat he might hang
on a hook with other missing coats.

The Mute, the Noise

Casting a shadow on the living room table,
the artist's model with his head bowed
and his hands by his sides
looks like he's asking for something:
palms upturned, blank-faced,
straight-faced, chastened,
he's here night after night:
silent occupant miming regret,
as might a human model—

Chorus

We didn't believe an elephant could squeeze into church
so we went to church and waited while the priest
kept saying *listen* and *forgive* and the animals all around us
listened, or didn't listen, some strained against leashes,
some wore disguises that made them look like people we knew,
people we should forgive or be forgiven by,
we didn't know which, even the elephant
looked like someone we knew, flooding the doorway
like a curtain of light, swaying from side to side.
Her hide was cracked down to her feet and her eyes,
they shone like glass before it breaks. She looked
like she might fly but only walked down the aisle
in a dirty gown of wrinkles, so wrinkled and slow
and vast and silvery, the whole galaxy shivering.

Chorus

Everyone asks what we're afraid of
but we aren't supposed to say.
We could put loneliness on the list.
We could put this list on the list,
its infinity. We could put infinity down.
Who knows why we're here, it's a "mystery."
We're getting older,
and when no one's watching
we climb right into it.

Chorus

The ones we love fall asleep
to our abandon,
we are always abandoning them
and then finding them,
we'd be lost could we not
abandon them, could we not
find and abandon them.

Tell no one where we go at night
in our sleep, how far we walk,
toward what, but accompany us
to the soundings, the quicksands,
and the rocks.

From the Doorway

The night is covered
in books and papers and child

and I like having him here,
sleeping loose and uninhibited.

The room fills with sleep
and the poor dummy heart

already straining at my seams
makes the tearing sound.

Fear. Or laughter.
Love,

the strangest
of all catastrophes.

Soliloquy

Why shouldn't I want to think of being here
even after the sun untouched by all theories
of evolution drags its implacable shadow
from behind the bleachers and lowers it
over our vast captive faces.

Endless Forms Most Beautiful

Praise these eyes for opening
before the highway split
and for giving the second another second,
another second or hours

or days in which, suddenly old enough
to sit beside me in the passenger seat,
doubled over, face in shadow,
the nape of his neck

exposed, the back of his head
more known and unknowable to me
than anything else on the skidding earth,
the child humming along with Z100's

You reached me at the right number but at the wrong time
can reach into the dirty footwell not to brace
for the irreparable but simply
to tighten his cleats, singing,

feeding the endless black laces
through the line of bright aluminum eyes.

Inventory

Down at the grocery store, tacked to the board,
flapping in the wind,
the business card says
"Husband 4 A Day."
She takes a few,
tucks them into May, then June,

but now it's August
and she says the boy can use them
as bookmarks, placeholders,
kindling. She'd still like a husband,
or at least a keepsake,
a light that switches on

when anyone comes near.
She'd like more books, fewer rocks,
a path in the woods.
At night she hears knocking
from the fields, something
undoes in the wind.

In the morning, the floors creak
and hum because what's gone
is also there, singing
inside the clutch of stones
the boy slingshots into air.

Prima Materia

He still doesn't believe in the soul,
so when I say again
marvel at the visible, he looks away
and closes his eyes
until practicing what not to say
and how not to say it

I don't tell him how his own eyes,
open or closed, bored, resigned,
consigned to his fate,
are extraordinary,
how even the vagrancies in their place
come to beauty there.

Chorus

The mothers keep promising clear skies
but when we look up
it's all clouded over, like a fortune-teller's face
in the face of the clouds.

We turn our own faces to the clouds
so the ones trying to hide from us
won't recognize who cries
to see them cry.

Which way? we say.
Onward, the clouds say.

Chorus

If only they wouldn't leave us so alone.
At the fair, and farther out, in the arcades,
in arcadia—

where with three darts for a dollar
we puncture every balloon
and like dimes

fling ourselves into the dime toss
the barkers lay before us.
What prize should we choose?

Where are we or where should we be?
Should be somewhere, we know that.
Prizes hang from every stall

and BB guns shout,
louder than we can shout.

Chorus

Whoever's calling keeps hanging up, he
won't leave a message—
so we brush the television, watch our teeth,
and pretend to go to bed,
listening for ringtones in our heads—

Chorus

Because it's closing time at the Houdini Museum
and because there are so many of us,
Bravo the Magician calls us all up on stage
and gives us bright red ribbons to wave.
He says we've seen enough straitjackets
for one Valentine's Day, says they belong
to Houdini, as do the handcuffs, and the posters,
but please not Dorothy Dietrich who's so beautiful
she makes us forget it's February outside
in Scranton, Pennsylvania.
Her silver sandals glitter in the lights.
She can catch a bullet in her mouth.
She's fearless enough to be a mother
but on stage she looks nothing like a mother.
The ribbons in our hands turn white.

Chorus

We thought it was safe under trees,
we thought the storm would end but it came down
harder over fields where there was no one to ask
but mothers and lightning and who was that coming from?
We were watching the sky and then what got lifted
into the sky. Leaves, trash,
a circle of dirt—

Then someone's scarf took to the sky,
the sky swallowed the scarf, red bird
floundering on a black pond,
red soaked with years of sweat
and then with storm,
red like a toy.

Chorus

Down at the lake,
the men who run the shack
pretend they're ministers

and maybe it's true.
Once, a dozen yards off shore,
playing tag in the warm lake water,

we called to them as if they could find us.
Marco! we said, our eyes closed,
until they said *Polo!*

But most days they stay in the back
counting their oars and canoes.
Their teeth are as white as their shirts,

their boats shallow and cheap.
For a pair of shoes and a set of keys,
they let us go out late, past closing,

they leave us to winds
that carry us beyond the pale swivel-eye buoys
into the smooth hard waters.

Sojourn

My son took a picture of me
jumping the cemetery wall. *Do it again,*
he said, as if I'd got out too fast.
Pretend you're really climbing.

In the retake my lazy eye is half shut,
and the other is smiling or crying.

Hangman

When did he start to play in reverse,
erasing the figures line by line until now
they're shadow and blank space and fragrance?
Sometimes he calls the vowels so quickly
it sounds like he's laughing,
erasing limb by limb,
finger by finger,
until only the word is left.

The Game of Boxes

All we need is time and a pen,
no words, no money, no one else
traversing the white field of ellipses

I draw all night
to distract my boy
from the greater deletions—

It's a simple game,
seven dots by seven, eight by eight:

there's no end to it,
nor to dust nor to snow.

Chorus

So who mothers the mothers
who tend the hallways of mothers,
the spill of mothers, the smell of mothers,
who mend the eyes of mothers,
the lies of mothers scared
to turn on lights in basements
filled with mothers called by mothers in the dark,
the kin of mothers, the gin of mothers,
mothers out on bail,
who mothers the hail-mary mothers
asleep in their stockings
while the crows sing heigh ho carrion crow,
fol de riddle, lol de riddle,
carry on, carry on—

Of All Faces

Sweet Double, Talk-Talk

i.

It's a different beauty.
Your torso is stained and creased,
you say you're an old man—

the backs of your hands
might be an old man's hands
but the tips of your fingers—

little shocks of pure mind,
and I like them there, yes, ageless,
persuasion's design and rush.

ii.

Forget what everyone says
about sex, how it makes us immortal.

I think maybe it only makes us
feel immortal.

Still, your pale blue stare—
puts this havoc in the air.

iii.

If you want I'll
cover you with my body.

I'll be a sheet draped over you,
the bone of my pelvis will press your tailbone.

I still smell something harmed,
but the knocking in my chest disappears

when I stretch my arms across yours.

iv.

I know agape means both dumbly
open and love not the kind of love
that climbed the stairs to you.

v.

Dressed:
elegant, formal, masked.

Undressed:
Who's more afraid, he asked.

vi.

Not just hands but all
urgencies: fingers, mouth,
the dirtiest things.

Now he's been inside me
he says he's better but I'm
ravenous. He lets me want,

touch, cry:
he's a lozenge of smut,
almost hollow inside.

vii.

He promised to hum in my ear
until I fell asleep—

I should have closed my eyes and listened,
I should stop listening,

it was just a tranquilizer,
what's the danger,

what's the danger
in being soothed, held,

letting the babydoll sleep?
Your voice fills my veins,

my mind, my restless
anatomical

slit—
hush babydoll, babydoll hush.

viii.

Sure, I say, fine, as if it doesn't matter
where he touches me.

And it does feel good to me,
a pleasure,

a match lifted from its neat white box
and struck on the afterlife bed.

I like the lights on low,
but he prefers night to be night.

ix.

I'd never been so thirsty,
and suddenly.

In the middle of the night I
climbed the steps to my hurt on his

and his on mine.
We poured the hot drink down.

x.

Beneath the oval mirror hanging from twine,
pale, urgent, abashed,

he didn't have to ask
do you like what you see

but only lull me with endearments
until my eyes don't wander.

xi.

Never will I say
ok, yes, so this is it,
this is love.

He's only homeopathy,
a little lust—
tincture, overdose,

vials of must—
"an outrage to human reason,"
nothing to trust.

xii.

Though I can't sleep neither could I wake,
and when you spoke I heard only the come-on
hard-on voice of *this is how I'll do it to you* so I moved away,
I wanted you to leave.
And I was scared again, or lonely,
because they were your socks knotted up in the bed,
your sweater draped on the back of my chair,
your clothes on my clothes, ardent, and spent.

xiii.

You say your mother's still here
but I'm the woman in the bed—

Lullaby, lullaby,
rockabye dread.

xiv.

Why do you say you love to bring me gifts
when all you give me
are a few sweet cherries in a black bag,
a bruised white peach?
Acetaminophen is no gift
and I'm glad it didn't work—
I like the fever
even after the fever broke.

xv.

O borrower thou,
devourer thou,

terrestrial thou make nice.
Don't call me thou,

don't tell me thou,
just play me now, like dice.

xvi.

So hurry up let it get late,
hurry up let it happen again,
the short cold night will end

but not the force of the mind
left dallying, straddling the extremes,
engine of want refueling itself on want,

on sweet talk, double-talk, cry—
sweet double, talk-talk, cry—

xvii.

Sometimes he's everything to me:
yesterday, tomorrow, regret and shame.

And sometimes he's nothing to me,
an old cushion on an old couch:

a pin-cushion:
something I think I can replace.

xviii.

I'm afraid you'll die,
and tonight's your birthday, it's no different,
in fact it's worse,
come drink some wine—

Let's sit at the bar.
It's winter,
so I'm in your coat,
I'm in your promises,
your smooth worn promises
sliding in and out of my own
love of death so slick
with want—

Soon, you say, your breath still warm in my ear.

xix.

Finally there's someone I might
and have and could one day
want again, or tarry—

I could tarry a man like him,
warily—
at the supermarket, at the corner store,

where the perishables, waiting to be touched
and taken home, keep
trembling.

xx.

This evening you said you'd be at the barbershop
getting your hair cut but I keep seeing you here
in the gallery of Spanish paintings
with the other chiaroscuros, teasing other furies.

xxi.

Of all faces in the world
I found one to take downriver—

I play the game of wanting
while holding very still.

Will he reappear?
Or is he just invisible, it being the night.

xxii.

I want to see his face.
I'll be at his door again,
I'll just stay five minutes,
his face is a clue to me but I don't know
what it means. *You're sad* I say when he isn't sad,
maybe he's thinking about leaving me, or dying,
skipping rocks across a grave
or swinging his legs at its edge,
but I don't cry, that was a little while ago,
eons and eons ago.

xxiii.

What's different between that man
and this woman? We're both tired,
naked, in the same bed

and she thinks she can soothe him
by laying her body over his
the way she's always done,
the way she's been taught:

Mama—sweetheart—cunt—

Wake me when you wake, I say
to his *Hold me while I sleep.*

xxiv.

Then he whispers *there, there* as if I were a child
and not a woman lying beside him

but what's wrong with that
it's late

death's hovering like the cap
hanging from the doorknob

he takes in hand
when he goes

where never has anyone
left so quietly

disentangling the desires of one
from the desires of another.

Is life like that?
How I slept then.

The Modern Period

Which System Is Most Miraculous?

Language, he said. Eyes, I said.
Or conception. Birth.
When he left I was forlorn,
as if something in my body
had said good-bye for a long time.
A blue glass broke but I can't throw it away.
There's room for it on the shelf.
Or there's no room.
I wonder if I'm too old for all this.
I'm as old as the police station!
Old as a handful of pennies saved in a sack.
Words still fortify me but the blue is better,
brighter, almost as bright as when it was first
removed from its tissue and passed
from hand to hand.

In the Cabinet of What's Expired

Salves, creams, dreams in their shiny metal tins:
the balm of yes
is now the balm of no—

But it's a pretty silver hope,
and I still swallow it—
I let it wash down my throat,

my chest,
down my desire vortex
to my smooth wild feet,

I let it wash my feet—

Apophasis at the All-Night Rite Aid

Not wanting to be alone
in the messy cosmology
over which I at this late hour
have too much dominion,
I wander the all-night uptown Rite Aid
where the handsome new pharmacist,
come midnight, shows me to the door
and prescribes the moon,
which has often helped before.

Soliloquy, ii

I could not be, even now, just particles of mist
but I might wish to be—
I couldn't be mist because mist
is airborne, mist doesn't wear black
and dirty up so many pages.
No mother is only mist.
Even my child tells me I'm scared and
in the same breath says I'm scared of
nothing. Depends how you define "nothing"—
I think it's a little shard of the whatnot
I keep trying to name.
An empty glass can be said to hold nothing.
Perhaps I was mist in a previous life,
maybe that's why I can't understand
these instructions. Or perhaps I'll
be, in my next life, mist. When did it
get so mysterious? This isn't me speaking
but the old gentle hiss of a slow glass
ship in a bottle on the sea.

The Beautiful Optician

I paid a little copay and waited my turn
under the lights. She wasn't wearing
her white coat today but she was the chart
of spaciousness, she had custody of my eyes
and of the way my eyes see.
She had my mother's hands
but she was not my mother.
My glasses broke as soon as I left her,
as if they had a mind of their own
and wanted her repairs. When I went back
and tried on the hundredth pair she said
those are the ones, yes, and held up
a mirror. Sometimes I leave my glasses at home
and ask my shadow to stand a distance away.
I don't always like what I see,
I'm a little afraid, the traffic lights
take so long to turn green. I tell none of this
to the beautiful optician,
who says the problem is all mine.

The Right Hemisphere

Late at night the mind quiets, or
when listening to Mozart. All the studies
say so, they show maps of the brain
when you're having chills listening
to something beautiful the way a man's cry
is beautiful to me I'm ashamed to say.
The part of the brain where music gets processed
is close to my memories of a few men
in flagrante, or whatever that is
when they open their mouths and cry out
and for a moment the brain lights up.
"Present," I might have said
though for most of those nights I wasn't,
not really. I wanted to be.
I don't like to think about the past,
I was afraid to say "here"
though there I was listening.

Inventory, ii

Really, what chance do any of us have
for moments of bliss? I knew where to find
the saddest people, but I was way too
somehow to stop for a friendly beep-beep.
But now I want to play here.
Oh to sit in a parked car with
other cars, and radios.
Look up!
Even the clouds wrangle for a little of their own—
The clouds give way and let us ride along in it.

Vast & Lonesomely

It comforts me to know the pharaohs yearned
to be young forever and arranged for boats
to carry them to the afterworld.

The only boat I have is the bed it takes me
too long to rise from, too long to return to.
The pomegranates in my house have softened,

the oranges go soft, the flowers
from Ilya darken and soften the water
that pulls through the pipes into

the clear glass vase of today,
a good day for sleeping,
a fascinating day.

Mornings,

the boy across the table seems illuminated,
a kind of man-angel in his white t-shirt
and not just an optical illusion
but real, the kind you can't wash out,
the kind that leads to cures or happiness,
like penicillin, or wine. I don't remember
putting one foot in front of the other
but we must have because here we are,
for another little while,
trying to make it to the intersection
of Pleasure and Meaning, which the map
says is a little further inside of here.

Still Life

The woman leaning against the window
is she here or across the street or far away?
It looks like she's already given herself to the world.

The Modern Period

When Gutenberg figured out
how to make letters that could be
rearranged he changed us all.

Once upon a time
I laid my head on books
and was surrounded by books

and bought books and rescued books
reminding me I had only
finite years in the book of my son,

whom I almost left for books,
to whom I leave my books.

Providence

This evening I shared a cab with a priest
who said it was a fine day to ride cross town

with a writer. But I can't
finish the play I said,

it's full of snow.
The jaywalkers

walked slowly, a cigarette warmed
someone's hand.

Some of the best sermons
don't have endings, he said

while the tires rotated unceasingly
beneath us.

All over town people were waiting
and doubleparked and

making love and waiting.
The temperature dropped

until the shiverers zipped their jackets
and all manner of things started up again.

Notes

The title "Endless Forms Most Beautiful" comes from Darwin's *The Origin of Species* and Richard Einhorn's oratorio, *The Origin*, where it is beautifully transformed into music.

"Chorus [We want to know the reasons]": "A little fortitude, a little patience" is inspired by Ralph Waldo Emerson's "Patience and fortitude conquer all things."

"Old Story" is for Eleanor Ross Taylor.

The title "Categories of Understanding" is borrowed from Kant's notion of categories.

"Chorus [The ones we love]": the phrase "The Soundings, the quicksands, & the rocks" is from Keats's letter to J.A. Hessey, 8 October 1818. For Carl Dennis.

"Endless Forms Most Beautiful": the line "You reached me at the right number but at the wrong time" is from the song "Don't Break My Heart" by B.o.B.

Prima Materia: the phrase "marvel at the visible" is from a talk given by Heather McHugh.

"The Game of Boxes" is in conversation with Robert Frost's "Dust of Snow."

"Sweet Double, Talk-Talk" part xi.: In 1843, Queen Victoria's physician, Sir John Forbes, denounced homeopathy, which was a relatively new and very controversial treatment; he called it "an outrage to human reason." Homeopathy works on the principle that, as the

Renaissance physician Paracelsus said, "What makes a man ill also cures him."

"Providence": "the shiverers" is from Emily Dickinson's 1862 poem [#335], "'Tis not that Dying hurts us so—"

Acknowledgments

With gratitude for the guidance, patience, friendship, and beautiful work of Jericho Brown, Leslie Bushara, Richard Einhorn, Alexandra Enders, Miranda Field, Saskia Hamilton, James Hoch, Susan Karwoska, Deborah Landau, Alessandra Lynch, Michael Morse, Dennis Nurkse, Kathleen Peirce, Claudia Rankine, Ed Skoog, Jean Valentine, Ellen Bryant Voigt, David Wells, Abigail Wender, Rynn Williams, and Eleanor Wilner. And for my family: my parents, my sisters, my brother, my son.

My deep and ongoing thanks to the Guggenheim Foundation and the Whiting Foundation for their support.

Appreciation to the editors of the *American Poetry Review, Gulf Coast,* the *Kenyon Review,* the *Literary Review,* and *TriQuarterly* for publishing some of these poems in earlier incarnations.

Catherine Barnett is the author of a previous collection of poems, *Into Perfect Spheres Such Holes Are Pierced*. She has received a fellowship from the Guggenheim Foundation and a Whiting Writers' Award. She works as an independent editor and teaches at the New School and New York University.

Composition by BookMobile Design and Digital Publisher Services, Minneapolis, Minnesota. Manufactured by Versa Press on acid-free 30 percent post-consumer wastepaper.